WITHDRAWN

SO-CFT-880

Jul 17 '73S	Aug2	
Sep 8 '7	Nov11'82SN	
Dec 11 '73S	Feb 17'83SN	
	Mar10'83SN	
Nov14 '74S	Mar31'83SN	
May12'75S	14'83SN	
May15'75S		
	Nov 3'83SN	
Aug28'75S	SNOHOMISH	
Feb23'76S		
Sep18'76S		
Nov20'76S		
Dec 4'76S		
Apr16'77S		
Jul31'78S		
May16'80S		
Jan16'81S		
May 5'8 S		
May28'81S		
Nov 6'81SN		

GAYLORD   PRINTED IN U.S.A.

JB   Aliki
PENN   The story of
ALIKI   William Penn
1964

3 9067 00257111 9

The Story Of
WILLIAM PENN

Written and Illustrated by *Aliki*

Prentice-Hall Inc., Englewood Cliffs, N.J.

2⊄2⊄⊄

The Story of William Penn by Aliki

© 1964 by Aliki Brandenberg

Copyright under International and Pan American Copyright Conventions

All rights reserved, including the right to reproduce this book, or any portions thereof, in any form, except for the inclusion of brief quotations in a review. Library of Congress Catalog Card Number: 64-14025

Printed in the United States of America   J-85044

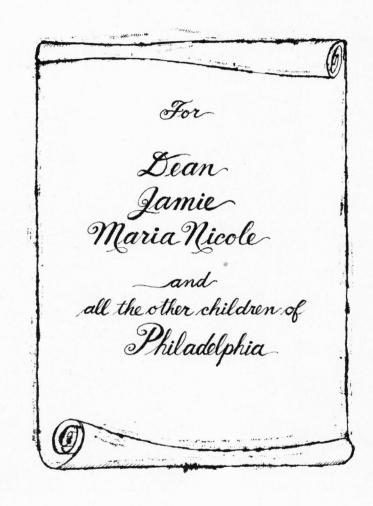

For

Dean
Jamie
Maria Nicole

and
all the other children of
Philadelphia

Snohomish Public Library

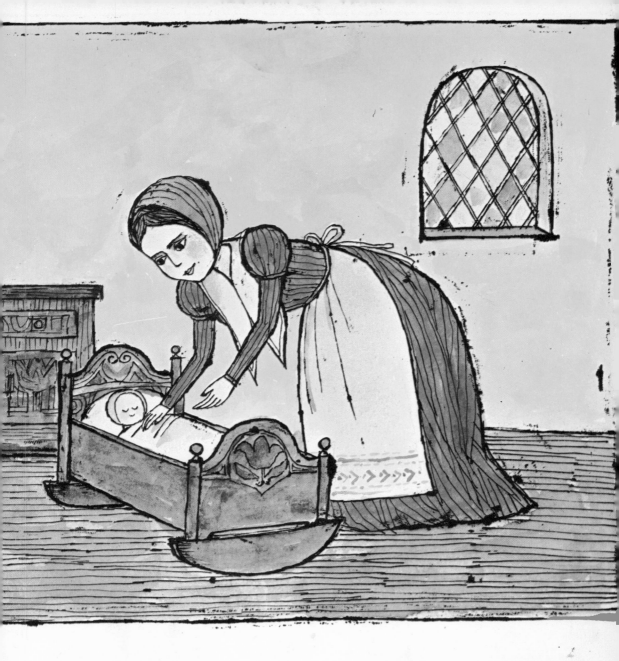

Many years ago there lived a man all the world
grew to know. His name was William Penn.

William lived in England with his wife and children,
whom he dearly loved.

His kindness and wisdom won William many friends. Some of them were plain people. Some were noble. One was the King of England himself.

Although William was wealthy, he did not choose the gay life of the rich. He wore no frills as they did. He was a simple man who admired others for their goodness, and not for what they owned.

William was a Quaker. The Quakers are gentle, peaceful people, and do not believe in fighting. They think that all men should live side by side as brothers.

But in those days, in England, people were not free to say what they chose. They had to speak carefully, or they were punished. Many, who would not obey, were sent to prison.

William Penn was not afraid. He spoke to the people and told them to believe as they wished. He wrote books and traveled to other countries, telling everyone of freedom.

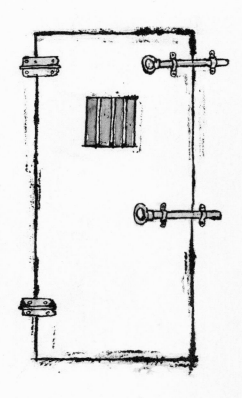

William, too, was sent to prison for a while because he spoke so freely. Yet he never lost his hope that all men could live together as brothers.

As the years passed, more and more people grew to know and love William Penn and to believe in his ideas.

Now the King happened to owe William a huge
sum of money. And when it was time for the King to pay
his debt, he decided to give William a large piece of land
in America, instead of money.

William had heard of the New World, and of those who went there to seek a better life. He had long dreamed of going there himself.

William set to work, finding people to go with him. He told them that in America they would be free to think and speak as they pleased.

William's new land was named Pennsylvania – the woods of Penn.

William planned where a city would be built and where its homes would be.

And he named it Philadelphia – the city of brotherly love.

Snohomish Public Library

When everything was ready, William bid his family
farewell, for they would join him later. The sails were
spread and the brave group left their homeland.

The journey was long. The ship moved slowly onward, rocking and tossing on the white-capped waves. Many people fell ill, and everyone wanted the voyage to end.

Two long months passed.

Then one day, they saw their new land. They saw wigwams nestled among the trees, and Indians watching them from a distance.

And on the shore stood some earlier settlers, who had come from afar to welcome them.

And they rejoiced.

But the Indians were uneasy. Many of their people had been chased from the land and hurt by other settlers.

William wanted to make friends with the Indians. He did not want them to be afraid of him and of his people, so he invited them to a meeting.

The Indians came, wearing their finest headdresses. The settlers and the Indians gave each other gifts in the shade of an old elm tree.

William Penn wrote a Peace Treaty which said:
In this land our two peoples will live
together in respect and freedom.

He proved to all the world that men can live as brothers, if they choose.

The Indians trusted William because he was fair to them. He did not chase them from their land, but bought it from them.

He visited their homes and respected their ways. He even learned to speak their language, and said it was the most beautiful language of all.

William's city grew. More homes were built,
and new settlers came in great numbers.

To this day, the father of Philadelphia looks down upon his people. And his people look up at him, with pride. ⫷⫷⫷